Gardens of the Heart

By Laurinda Wallace

Sierra Vista, AZ

Gardens of the Heart

©2012 Laurinda Wallace

ISBN: 978-0-9854328-4-3

Cover Design by C. D. Davis

Cover image by Celwell

Interior Photos and Author Photo by Jesaro Photography

Scripture quotations marked (NLT) are taken from the Holy Bible, New Living Translation, copyright © 1996, 2004, 2007 by Tyndale House Foundation. Used by permission of Tyndale House Publishers, Inc., Carol Stream, Illinois 60188. All rights reserved.

Scriptures taken from the Holy Bible, New International Version®, NIV®. Copyright © 1973, 1978, 1984, 2011 by Biblica, Inc.™ Used by permission of Zondervan. All rights reserved worldwide. www.zondervan.com

Scripture taken from the NEW AMERICAN STANDARD BIBLE®, Copyright © 1960,1962,1963,1968,1971,1972,1973,1975,1977,1995 by The Lockman Foundation. Used by permission.

ALL RIGHTS RESERVED

No part of this publication may be reproduced, stored in a retrieval system, or transmitted, in any form or by any means—electronic, mechanical, photocopying, recording, or otherwise—without prior written permission.

For information contact:

3-MICE PRODUCTIONS ♦ PO Box 415 ♦ Hereford, AZ 85615

For my mother, Fay

and

my grandmothers, Marguerite and Margaret

God's Garden

Then the LORD God planted a garden in Eden in the east, and there he placed the man he had made. The LORD God placed the man in the Garden of Eden to tend and watch over it.

Genesis 2:8, 15 NLT

What a simple plan! God planted the Garden of Eden and placed the man He'd made in His own image to care for it. This was before weeds, before thorns, before the curse of sin. It was perfect and the task wasn't too strenuous.

From the very beginning, we see that our Creator delights in growing a garden. The garden was meant for us to enjoy. God designed the first one and planted it Himself, just for us. However, it didn't take Adam and Eve long to ruin their perfect life in Eden. Now gardening requires more effort and is often frustrating because of the weeds, the imperfect soil, and bad weather conditions. Still, there's much beauty to be found in gardening, which restores our souls and strengthens our arms. Working the ground and getting our hands dirty can chase a bad day away.

Even if spading up the ground isn't high on your list of pleasant tasks, that bouquet of flowers on the kitchen counter or African violet in the window can bring a smile. It's a natural connection to the One who designed us with such care and love.

The garden He wants you to tend and watch over today isn't a vegetable patch or a flowerbed, but the garden that's in your heart. Is yours an arid desert? A rocky, hard place or filled with weeds? A rich loamy heart, fully given to Jesus Christ, is what He wants for each of us. To cultivate that kind of heart garden, we need to stay in His Word and close to Him. Today is the first day we begin tending that garden.

❦In the Garden❦ *When beginning a new vegetable or flower garden, consider placement according to how much sun and shade it will receive. Vegetables need full sun, as do many flowers, but there are lots of flowers that prefer shade.*

It's All About the Soil

He told many stories in the form of parables, such as this one: "Listen! A farmer went out to plant some seeds. As he scattered them across his field, some seeds fell on a footpath, and the birds came and ate them.

Matthew 13:3-4 NLT

The seed that fell on the footpath represents those who hear the message about the Kingdom and don't understand it. Then the evil one comes and snatches away the seed that was planted in their hearts.

Matthew 13:19 NLT

Every gardener knows you need the right soil to grow anything. Whether it's a flower, vegetable, or even a weed, the wrong soil can't grow any of them well or sometimes even grow them at all.

There's a path through the front yard that winds around some mesquite trees and ends out by the dirt road we live on. The path was made by some strange pig-like animals called javelina, which frequent our yard at night. Their small hooves have packed down the red dirt until it's rock hard. Not even stubborn tumbleweed could grow on that path. It can't take root.

Jesus explained what He meant when He talked about the seed that was thrown on the path. The seeds of truth had no opportunity to take root because Satan snatched it away immediately. The heart that lacks understanding is like a well-worn path. Truth lies vulnerable to immediate attack and is easily taken away before it can make a difference. The heart remains dry and dusty—indifferent to the life giving truth of the gospel.

Possibly your own heart is hardened to the truth of God's Word. Have you allowed Satan to snatch away the Good News of Jesus Christ? Do you regularly spend time in God's Word? Soften your heart to God's truth today and let the message of the Kingdom change your life.

◈In the Garden◈ *Work in rich compost to break up heavy clay soil. The compost will add needed nutrients, and help with moisture retention and drainage.*

Shallow Ground

Other seeds fell on shallow soil with underlying rock. The seeds sprouted quickly because the soil was shallow. But the plants soon wilted under the hot sun, and since they didn't have deep roots, they died.

Matthew 13:5-6 NLT

The seed on the rocky soil represents those who hear the message and immediately receive it with joy. But since they don't have deep roots, they don't last long. They fall away as soon as they have problems or are persecuted for believing God's word.

Matthew 13:20-21 NLT

Rocky soil is a real pain. Every year before we planted our vegetable garden, we had to uncover stones in the garden plot, and toss them on a wagon. I didn't see the need for that annual preparation as a ten-year-old, but when I had my own gardens as an adult, it made perfect sense. They got in the way of my hoe and tiller. More importantly, those rocks hindered the root system of any seeds or plants we put in the ground.

Tomato plants wouldn't last in the summer heat if their roots weren't deep enough. They wouldn't have the sturdy foundation to withstand wind or a heavy thunderstorm. The plant can be washed out, wither and die, or blow over. It doesn't grow to maturity if it's planted in rocky ground. The tomato plant may look like it's doing great, but when some hot weather comes along; it doesn't have the strength to get through it.

Are your roots deep enough in God's Word to withstand life's problems? Are you ready to cave when someone questions your faith?

Paul told Timothy to "carefully guard the precious truth that has been entrusted to you," in 2 Timothy 1:14. Don't give up! Allow the Father to help you get rid of the rocks so that you will have the deep roots to stand up against life's problems and speak the truth.

In the Garden *Plan to regularly turn over the soil in your vegetable garden to expose the larger rocks. It'll help both the plants and maintenance time.*

Choking on Weeds

Other seeds fell among thorns that grew up and choked out the tender plants.

Matthew 13:7 NLT

The seed that fell among the thorns represents those who hear God's word, but all too quickly the message is crowded out by the worries of this life and the lure of wealth, so no fruit is produced.

Matthew 13:22 NLT

Have you ever planted a new flower or a vegetable plant in a bed of weeds? Probably not. It would be pointless and harm the good plant. Jesus talked about the seed that fell among the thorns and had no place to grow. The thorns took over and effectively killed the young seedlings. When I put a new plant into the ground, I make sure that there are no weeds around so it has every chance of surviving and doing well. That's part of soil preparation.

It's the same thing when we crowd our lives with the world's priorities—the pursuit of stuff, worry about what we're going to wear, how we're going to fit in one more appointment, one more errand. It's like a hamster on a wheel. We have too much activity and too little today. There is no room for God's Word or any time with Him. We keep ourselves busy and have no time for the relationship that matters most. Because we fill our days to overflowing, our spiritual life becomes choked out. In no time at all, we don't have time for Bible study, worship, or even a quick prayer. We were never intended to live this way. Our Heavenly Father wants us to live a balanced life, one that has room to breathe and grow.

Clearing the weeds from an old vegetable patch gives my young, tender pepper plants an excellent spot to grow. It's a place where their roots can spread out; grow deep, and their leaves branch out strong and tall without competition from noxious weeds and invasive roots. Take a hard look at your schedule and clear the weeds away by making time with the Savior and in His Word. Find balance, the right priorities, and grow deep roots in Him.

❧**In the Garden**❧ *Keeping up with weeds and pulling them out before they go to seed means less weeds next year. It's a great motivation for weeding regularly.*

The Good Soil

Still other seeds fell on fertile soil, and they produced a crop that was thirty, sixty, and even a hundred times as much as had been planted!

Matthew 13:8 NLT

The seed that fell on good soil represents those who truly hear and understand God's word and produce a harvest of thirty, sixty, or even a hundred times as much as had been planted!"

Matthew 13:23 NLT

Loamy, dark moist soil—a gardener's dream. No stones, weeds or clay, just rich dirt that will allow the plant to reach its full potential whether it's tomatoes, delphiniums, or strawberries. The harvest Jesus is talking about isn't meager; it's rich—a hundred, sixty or thirty times what was actually sown. Arizona dirt leaves a lot to be desired in the loamy department, so I've learned to appreciate that good soil from Back East in a whole new way.

The heart that has good soil is one who willingly and joyfully receives God's Word and does something with it. It's a life that shares the bounty of what they have, gives an encouraging word, lends a hand to their neighbor, and shows up at the church on a workday. A life that touches others because it's a visible expression of Christ's love everywhere it goes. It's a productive life that goes way beyond what you or I can imagine. A Kingdom of God kind of life. And it's entirely possible for each of us if we decide with the Father's help to be loamy, fertile soil.

Enriching your heart and relationship with God at an even deeper level is taking some time to retreat away from everyday activities. Take your Bible, journal, pen, and coffee to the backyard or a park. Spend some uninterrupted time with your Heavenly Father. Will you take the time to enrich your relationship with the Savior?

In the Garden *Most soils need amendment of some kind. Contact your local Cooperative Extension or Master Gardener program to have soil tested and find out what needs to be added.*

Planting or Watering?

It's not important who does the planting, or who does the watering. What's important is that God makes the seed grow. The one who plants and the one who waters work together with the same purpose. And both will be rewarded for their own hard work.

1 Corinthians 3:7-8 NLT

At our house, gardening is an equal opportunity task. It's a team effort. As long as the seeds get put in the ground and everything is watered sufficiently, it doesn't matter who does it. The goal is to have seeds grow, to give us chubby squash or crunchy lettuce.

The Corinthian church was in a competition with each other for bragging rights in ministry. How sad, but it's still true today. We sometimes do the same to draw attention to "our" ministry. We glibly talk about "my" childcare ministry. Then we get offended and lash out at our brothers and sisters in Christ when "our" ministry isn't given enough recognition or lacks workers. Andrew Murray said, "How much Christian work is being done in the spirit of the flesh and the power of self?" It's a good question.

We all need to grow up and work together. The command from Jesus is the same to every Christian—share the gospel and then disciple believers. There isn't a contest for "World's Greatest Ministry." God alone increases the harvest and He will reward each of us for our work done in His Name. Rather than critiquing ministries, take time to encourage fellow laborers this week and don't get caught up in a fleshly contest.

☙**In the Garden**☙ *Tomato plants should be started inside during the late winter. Old egg cartons can be repurposed as seedling starters. When the plants outgrow the starter containers, they can be repotted in peat pots and hardened off before planting in the garden after the danger of frost is past.*

Peaceful Planters

But the wisdom from above is first of all pure. It is also peace loving, gentle at all times, and willing to yield to others. It is full of mercy and good deeds. It shows no favoritism and is always sincere. And those who are peacemakers will plant seeds of peace and reap a harvest of righteousness.

James 3:17-18 NLT

When watering the vegetable garden, I don't withhold water from one tomato over another. I water all of them. It's the same with the flowers. The roses and honeysuckle are fed and watered without favoritism. The reward is beautiful flowers and lots of tomatoes.

The world's concept of wisdom is vastly different from God's. While much worldly wisdom is directed at getting ahead and promoting our own agendas, godly wisdom is about character. It's about our behavior and controlling our tongues. When we're planting seeds of ambition and greed to scramble to the top of the pile, eventually someone else will come along and climb over us.

When we plant seeds of peace, we're investing in other people's lives to meet needs, to help them get ahead. The top of the pile has very little meaning when we "honor one another above ourselves." (Romans 12:10b)

But the seeds of peace won't produce the righteous harvest if it's not sincere. Lots of people are doing good deeds, but the motivation is wrong. They want to be noticed for their charitable acts.

True wisdom is always sincere and isn't concerned if someone sees that kind act. It is always noticed by our Heavenly Father. How will you sow seeds of peace today?

❧In the Garden❧ *Mix a small amount of sand in with tiny seeds such as carrots to help in distributing them evenly in the row. There will be fewer plants to thin out later, which means a larger crop.*

Procrastination Problems

Farmers who wait for perfect weather never plant. If they watch every cloud, they never harvest.

Ecclesiastes 11:4 NLT

Are you someone who hesitates, waiting for perfect conditions to get a job done? Have you said, "Once the weather turns warmer, or colder, or when Christmas is over I'll organize the closet, start that diet, begin a regular quiet time"? We're all guilty at one time or another of putting off tasks. If it's a regular habit, it's a problem. Conditions will never be perfect to start or finish anything. It's like the couple who waits until they have enough money to have a baby. What's enough money? Most of our reasons for not doing something are pretty lame. We excuse ourselves when we know we should have a regular quiet time and we should lose weight to be healthier. Why is it so difficult? Fear plays a big role in procrastination. We're afraid of failure. Guess what! We all fail and have to start over many times in life. Solomon tells us that the person who waits for perfect conditions never accomplishes anything.

God understands our weaknesses, but He expects us to ask for help when we're faced with difficult or even tedious tasks. Paul says in Philippians, "I can do all things through Christ who gives me strength." Through Christ. He is the one who is strong and wants us to succeed. It's only by His strength that we accomplish anything. What are you afraid of beginning? It doesn't matter how big the task or goal is, Jesus stands ready to help. You only have to ask. What are you waiting for?

❦In the Garden❦ *Vegetables that can tolerate colder temperatures can be planted earlier than more tender varieties. Greens, peas, and beets are early starters. String beans, corn, and squash should be planted after the danger of frost is past.*

Gardens of the Heart

Sowing Generously

Remember this—a farmer who plants only a few seeds will get a small crop. But the one who plants generously will get a generous crop. You must each decide in your heart how much to give. And don't give reluctantly or in response to pressure. "For God loves a person who gives cheerfully." And God will generously provide all you need. Then you will always have everything you need and plenty left over to share with others. As the Scriptures say, "They share freely and give generously to the poor. Their good deeds will be remembered forever." For God is the one who provides seed for the farmer and then bread to eat. In the same way, he will provide and increase your resources and then produce a great harvest of generosity in you. 2 Corinthians 9:6-10 NLT

I love looking down rows of lettuce and other greens that are chockfull of nice healthy plants. Then there's the sight and scent of the Lincoln rosebush when there are lots and lots of fragrant, deep red blooms. It's lavish and extravagant in the garden world.

If you want a lot of carrots, you don't plant five or six seeds; you plant a lot of seeds. Maybe a couple of packets of seeds even. If you want lots of roses, you feed and water liberally. It's only logical.

What's true in the garden is true with our money. Ouch! It's a touchy subject for most people. We come up with all sorts of excuses not to give to the church, the poor, or help out with a need. Giving our money generously to God comes with a lot of big promises. First, you'll have all you need and more to share if you give generously. Generous giving is remembered forever—not just with a plaque in the church hallway or a mention in the bulletin, but it's laying up treasure in heaven.

What we give is between God and us, although the tithe (the first 10% of earnings) is a good place to start. The Lord has given us jobs to meet our financial needs. We need to recognize that provision with a cheerful, giving heart. How would lives be changed, including our own if we gave cheerfully and generously?

❧In the Garden❧ *Before today's machinery, farmers sowed seed by "broadcasting." They took handfuls of seed and walked through the tilled fields, throwing it over the ground. They were able to cover larger areas with this ancient method.*

Gardens of the Heart

Weed Seeds

A troublemaker plants seeds of strife; gossip separates the best of friends.

Proverbs 16:28 NLT

Gardens of the Heart

Do you know someone who loves to stir up trouble? They enjoy passing on a comment from a co-worker to watch the fireworks. Maybe a family member just can't seem to let go of the past. He or she has to get a dig in at every family gathering. Or sometimes it's betraying a confidence, like sharing a friend's prayer request in the name of Christianity.

We justify it by saying more people could pray about the issue. One thoughtless or cruel remark can crush someone or tear apart a relationship. Those are seeds of strife that cause pain and destroy lives. Once the words are said, even a longstanding friendship can be harmed, sometimes irreparably.

Christian, stay away from people who delight in stirring the pot. Keep a close guard on your mouth. Don't indulge in tearing others down or spilling the beans on a friend who's confided in you. Use your speech for good and not for evil. Encourage someone today and smile. If you've been sowing bad seeds, stop.

With God's help speak only what is encouraging and positive. Watch your family and friends respond to good seeds. You'll want to make it habit.

❦In the Garden❦ A fun and easy inside garden project for children is to grow a mini pizza garden, by planting basil and oregano seeds in clay pots. The herbs grow quickly and soon you'll be able to snip fresh herbs to put on pizzas or use in spaghetti sauce.

Tiny Seeds—Big Results

"You don't have enough faith," Jesus told them. "I tell you the truth, if you had faith even as small as a mustard seed, you could say to this mountain, 'Move from here to there,' and it would move. Nothing would be impossible.

Matthew 17:20 NLT

A familiar saying is "mighty oaks from little acorns grow." Jesus used a similar observation with the mustard plant. If you've ever encountered whole mustard seeds in the spice section of the grocery store, you know that they are tiny yellow seeds, smaller than BB's. However, those tiny seeds produce a healthy sized shrub that can reach ten feet high in the Galilee region. Birds can certainly rest in its branches. What a great visual of a growing faith!

Just as the tiny oak seedling taking root in the mossy forest floor, our faith grows over time as we place more trust in God and His Word. Sometimes faith has a growth spurt through an experience and sometimes it suffers a setback. It is our choice to trust God or not. Even if your faith seems microscopic, it can grow and develop into a mature tree that provides rest and shelter for others.

What problem are you trying to handle yourself? Do you have more faith in yourself to handle it, rather than God? Take whatever it is to the Throne of Grace to find real help. Leave the issue with the Father and see how trustworthy He is.

☙In the Garden☙ *Poppy seeds are tiny. They look like black pepper in your hand. There are many varieties of these happy self-seeding flowers. To share your poppies, cut the seed heads about four or five inches down the stalk, tie together and hang upside down to dry. Once dry, shake the seeds onto a paper towel and share with friends.*

Infestation

For the locusts covered the whole country and darkened the land. They devoured every plant in the fields and all the fruit on the trees that had survived the hailstorm. Not a single leaf was left on the trees and plants throughout the land of Egypt.

Exodus 10:15 NLT

One fall, grasshoppers came in hoards to our area and chomped everything in sight. They were especially fond of iris and chewed the leaves into ribbons. Everywhere we walked, grasshoppers jumped and scattered ahead of us. They were a plague—on plants, the patio, on my shoes. Yuck! Maybe you've experienced some sort of infestation in your garden, whether it was insects or disease. It's sad to see the aftermath of such an event. Not only the loss of plants, but how stark and scarred the landscape is.

The plague of locusts was one of God's judgments on Pharaoh and the people of Egypt. The judgments got worse as Pharaoh's ego and stubbornness grew until it cost his son's life. Not only was the vegetation destroyed, but the people of Egypt experienced great suffering and loss.

Judgment isn't pretty. I'm not suggesting that God is judging you if grasshoppers have mowed down your flower garden or you've experienced tragedy. But Egypt's devastation so long ago reminds us of how serious God's judgment is and will be. The hard and stubborn heart isn't one that can please God. Persistent disobedience leads to a barren life, but the submissive and obedient heart towards God leads to abundant life.

In the Garden *A good bug in your garden is the ladybug. They feed on bad insects such as aphids, mites, and whiteflies. Plant daisies, tansy, or yarrow to attract ladybugs so they'll take up residence in the garden.*

Houseplants

So let's stop condemning each other. Decide instead to live in such a way that you will not cause another believer to stumble and fall.

          Romans 14:13 NLT

It is better not to eat meat or drink wine or do anything else if it might cause another believer to stumble.

          Romans 14:21 NLT

African violets just aren't outside plants. Neither are peace lilies or orchids. They would never survive the harsh winter season. We keep them in beautiful pots inside and maybe expose them to some fresh air and sun in a sheltered spot during warm weather. These plants need extra care and protection from the elements.

It's the same for many believers who are new to the faith or are immature in Christ. They aren't able to understand the freedom we have in Christ. They may be concentrating on keeping rules they've heard from others such as "Christians don't do _____." Just fill in the blank. For the early church, the frequent stumbling block was Jewish traditions. Even though we are certain the activity isn't sinful and doesn't contradict Scripture, it may cause a weaker brother or sister to stumble. Rather than condemning them for their lack of knowledge or faith, it is better to take the time to understand where they're coming from and be sensitive enough to deny ourselves in order to strengthen them. Yes, they need to grow stronger in understanding God's Word, but maybe it's an opportunity to invite them to a Bible study or encourage them in their Christian walk. As the more mature Christian, we need to take the high road with grace and love.

❧In the Garden❧ *African violets are an easy houseplant to grow. They like lots of indirect light, good drainage, and food made especially for them. To start a violet for a friend, snip off a healthy leaf and put it in a cup of water until it roots. Once it's well rooted, pot it until new leaves begin to appear. Then tie a bow around the pot and give it away.*

Soaking Rain

Confess your sins to each other and pray for each other so that you may be healed. The earnest prayer of a righteous person has great power and produces wonderful results. Elijah was as human as we are, and yet when he prayed earnestly that no rain would fall, none fell for three and a half years! Then, when he prayed again, the sky sent down rain and the earth began to yield its crops.

James 5:16-18 NLT

"We need a good soaking rain," my Dad would say when an occasional dry spell hit in the summer. Our big vegetable garden exhibited drought on withering leaves, small squash, and shriveled corn stalks. The effects of little or no rain are quickly evident on vegetable plants that need consistent and deep watering. The crops they produce are mostly water after all. Even if you water the garden with a hose, there's nothing like rainwater to bring on quick growth and good crop yields. Rain has all the right ingredients for plants.

A good rain is like effective prayer. It's pure and powerful. But sin holds back the blessings that our Heavenly Father wants to pour out on us. Even though Elijah was just an ordinary man, he prayed extraordinary things and God answered those prayers. His prayers weren't hindered.

When we don't seek forgiveness for harsh words or rude behavior from those we've hurt, drought can hit our prayer life. If we're not confessing our sins to God, who promises to forgive us, we're headed for drought too. Confession and forgiveness bring the rainclouds. Enjoy standing in a good soaking rain from heaven.

◈In the Garden◈ *If rainwater is a precious commodity in your area, or if you want to reduce consumption of water, check into rainwater harvesting from your roof. There are many options available and hundreds of gallons of rainwater can be collected to water the garden.*

Gardens of the Heart

From Eden to Gethsemane

They went to the olive grove called Gethsemane, and Jesus said, "Sit here while I go and pray." He took Peter, James, and John with him, and he became deeply troubled and distressed. He told them, "My soul is crushed with grief to the point of death. Stay here and keep watch with me." He went on a little farther and fell to the ground. He prayed that, if it were possible, the awful hour awaiting him might pass him by. "Abba, Father," he cried out, "everything is possible for you. Please take this cup of suffering away from me. Yet I want your will to be done, not mine."

Mark 14:32-36 NLT

The Creator of the universe planted a perfect garden in Eden for Adam and Eve to enjoy. He walked in the garden with them every evening. Then they believed Satan's lie and their relationship with God was broken. They lost the garden. The Creator came back to this sin-filled earth to rescue us and as He finished his earthly ministry, it was in another garden—the Garden of Gethsemane.

Jesus knew what faced him in the next few hours. He would be arrested. He would be beaten and spit upon. He would be accused by the religious leaders of his day, who would lie through their teeth about him. And then he would be nailed to a cross and hung to die like a common criminal. It was all for you, and it was all for me. Jesus didn't run away and he didn't give up, even though his most trusted disciples deserted Him. He could have said it wasn't worth it. He knew full well how wicked and selfish we really are. Jesus was still obedient to the Father's perfect plan to save us from our sins even though we most assuredly did not deserve it.

His sacrifice provides the only way to a restored relationship with God. It is eternal life—there is much more to come after life here on earth. His resurrection guarantees we will get back to the perfect garden of God, which Revelation 22 tells us is where the River of Life flows and fruit is always in season. Will you be there? Have you received His gift of eternal life?

☙**In the Garden**❧ *Take some time to spend with God in your garden today. There are so many things to be thankful for as we observe His complex and amazing creation. Most of all thank Him for the gift of His Son.*

Overtaken by Weeds

I walked by the field of a lazy person, the vineyard of one with no common sense. I saw that it was overgrown with nettles. It was covered with weeds, and its walls were broken down. Then, as I looked and thought about it, I learned this lesson: A little extra sleep, a little more slumber, a little folding of the hands to rest—then poverty will pounce on you like a bandit; scarcity will attack you like an armed robber.

Proverbs 24:30-34 NLT

Gardens of the Heart

The lawns of the old Georgian-style house swept down to a fieldstone wall by a quiet country road. Brilliant pink rhododendrons banked the foundation of the house. A formal English garden with an elaborate birdbath graced one side of the lawn. Sounds beautiful, right? It was, at one time. The gardens were sadly overgrown with weeds, the once lovely brick paths almost erased by encroaching grasses. The stone was crumbling, leaving gaps in the wall that surrounded the property. Somewhere along the way, the owner of the property gave up on maintaining the beauty that had taken so much work to establish.

Solomon observed the same thing in the vineyard of the lazy person. By neglecting the work of maintaining the vineyard, the person lost income from the crop. He was also on a path to poverty by ignoring the stewardship of the vineyard and most likely other areas of his life.

God expects us to be good stewards of the earthly things we've been given—homes, jobs, possessions, money. If we begin neglecting one area, it won't be long before we think other areas require too much effort to maintain. We aren't to worship or put these things in place of God, but we do need to recognize them as gifts. Good stewardship requires time, effort, and perseverance. Sometimes we need help in managing the blessings. Has your life been overtaken by weeds? Are your finances in a mess? Does the lawn need mowing? Are dishes piled in the sink? Are you overburdened with activity that keeps you from being a good steward of your blessings? Begin today to show your appreciation to your generous Father by caring for all that He's given you.

In the Garden *Mulch is an effective way to keep the weeds away in your flowerbeds. Two or three inches of fine bark mulch will keep it looking great with much less effort. It also helps keep soil moist, so you can water less.*

Tree of Life

The fruit of the righteous is a tree of life, and he who wins souls is wise.

Proverbs 11:30 NIV

If you were going to choose a tree of life in nature, the olive tree is a good choice. Not only does it produce olives, but that wonderful healthy olive oil is pressed from the fruit, the leaves are used in medicinal teas, and there is research into the development of an efficient and renewable energy source from the waste produced by oil pressings.

It was an olive leaf carried by the dove to Noah that brought hope to the weary residents of the ark. The olive branch is also the familiar symbol for peace we use today.

Olive trees have long lives and there are some trees in the Garden of Gethsemane that are believed to date back to the time of Jesus. The olive tree isn't impressive in size or particularly beautiful, but it's tough, productive, and has loads of character.

And that's what we need to be. It doesn't matter what we look like or where we're planted, but it does matter what our heart looks like and what we produce. If we're a tree of life that extends kindness, love, and mercy, that fruit will draw people to the Lord Jesus.

He stands ready to help you produce good fruit. Will you be wise and live with purpose, exhibiting Christ today?

❧In the Garden❧ *Herbs like basil, thyme, and rosemary are easy to grow and adds lots of flavor to many dishes. Instead of using butter on bread, dip it in extra virgin olive oil flavored with snips of fresh herbs like rosemary or basil.*

Romance in the Garden

Bride: "I am the rose of Sharon, The lily of the valleys."

Groom: "Like a lily among the thorns, So is my darling among the maidens."

Bride: "Like an apple tree among the trees of the forest, So is my beloved among the young men. In his shade I took great delight and sat down, And his fruit was sweet to my taste. He has brought me to his banquet hall, And his banner over me is love."

Song of Solomon 2:1-4 NASB

If your marriage needs a little romance, try reading the Song of Solomon. The magnificent imagery of this garden isn't about work, but about enjoying the garden. What beautiful words the bride and groom say to each other—enough to make us blush!

There will always be plenty of work to do, but time together whether it's over dinner, taking a walk, or in the bedroom is actually sacred. Marriage is the picture of Christ and the Church. Paul says in Ephesians that "This is a great mystery, but it is an illustration of the way Christ and the church are one." These two relationships are the most intimate we will ever have. They are both to be enjoyed and developed.

The first marriage began in a perfect garden. When Adam and Eve sinned, breaking their relationship with God, the first marital argument occurred. Marriage has been difficult ever since, but it's not impossible to keep romance kindled. It requires time, commitment, and a sense of humor. Respect and sacrifice are also essential components of marriage.

Make a date with your spouse to enjoy the garden—a moonlit walk, a special dinner, use your imagination. It's well worth the effort and it's one of the best investments you'll ever make.

In the Garden *Fragrant flowers like stock, lily-of-the-valley, lilacs, and roses add a special dimension to the flower garden. The sweet scents in the evening air are quite romantic. Make sure you plant a few where you can enjoy them.*

The Meadow

He lets me rest in green meadows; he leads me beside peaceful streams. He renews my strength. He guides me along right paths, brings honor to his name.

Psalm 23:2-3 NLT

The Shepherd King learned about the restorative properties of God's creation early in life. As a boy, David spent many long hours watching over his father's sheep in the rugged areas outside of Bethlehem. Those long days allowed him to spend time with God, learn to be still, and also creative in his music. He honed his slingshot skills, which would prepare him to face Goliath.

With cellphones attached to our ears, social media taking our every moment, we lose valuable time connecting with our Creator. We don't know how to be still and enjoy His presence. We insist that we just don't have the time to read the Bible, think about God, memorize Scripture, or pray. Isn't it strange that we devote our schedules to lots of activity that has nothing to do with developing our relationship with the Savior and we say it's more important?

Our frazzled and hectic lives would drastically change if we reordered our priorities, and followed Him beside peaceful streams. However, as busy as we are, it's not impossible to change and allow God to shape His heart into ours. It's our choice though and He never forces Himself on us. David made the choice to follow God early in life.

What are you missing out on by not devoting time to your Creator, Savior, Friend? It's not too late to start today.

☙In the Garden☙ *Shut off your electronic devices and enjoy some time with God today. Find a park or a quiet place in your yard or neighborhood to soak in the silence. Disconnect from the world and connect with God.*

Tangled Up

Therefore, since we are surrounded by such a huge crowd of witnesses to the life of faith, let us strip off every weight that slows us down, especially the sin that so easily trips us up. And let us run with endurance the race God has set before us.

Hebrews 12:1 NLT

Animals of all sorts visit my garden daily. Rabbits and birds are the most frequent visitors. They're not always welcome because of their sometimes destructive habits, but I do enjoy watching their antics, which often brings Scripture to mind.

One year, the birds were especially naughty and helped themselves to our crop of almost-ripe tomatoes. In an effort to keep them from ruining all those tasty globes, netting was stapled to a frame and placed over the plants in the large wooden tub.

One afternoon I found a rabbit hopelessly trapped in the trailing net. My husband immediately came to his rescue. Wearing heavy work gloves, he gently held the terrified rabbit and cut away the netting that entangled his leg. The rabbit struggled against his help, but was finally set free to find his mate who was hiding in a nearby mesquite thicket.

The rabbit's predicament is a reminder that it's easy to walk into the trap of sin. The NIV uses the word "entangles" in Hebrews 12:1, which gives us a great picture of what sin does to Christians who are supposed to be running a race. Have you ever gotten your feet wrapped up in a length of rope or tripped over a rock that landed you on the ground? It's hard to keep running if you're sitting in a heap.

It's time to get rid of the net and get back in the race. What sin trips you up? Are you ready and willing to cut away the net so you can run again?

❧**In the Garden**❧ *Water tomatoes regularly. Sporadic watering will cause the fruit to crack or they can develop blossom end rot.*

Prickly Disposition

Instead, be kind to each other, tenderhearted, forgiving one another, just as God through Christ has forgiven you.

Ephesians 4:32 NLT

And so blessing and cursing come pouring out of the same mouth. Surely, my brothers and sisters, this is not right! Does a spring of water bubble out with both fresh water and bitter water?

James 3:10, 11 NLT

There are many varieties of cactus, and the blooms are gorgeous. There's even a cactus that blooms for one night and then it's over. Called the Night Blooming Cereus or Queen of the Night, it produces a spectacular white star-like flower. The Claret Cup is another showy variety with deep red cup-like blooms.

Despite their beauty, as everyone knows, there's a very specific problem with cacti. It's their nasty thorns. And not all thorns are the same. Some have wicked long ones that are easy to see and some have more subtle thorns. They're small and even look like a soft fuzzy covering on some of the paddles. Don't be fooled! Those are some of the worst kind. Once on your hand, they quickly work their way underneath the skin, making it almost impossible to get them out. If you live in the desert, you learn to keep a safe distance from these succulents. There are other succulents that are thornless. One of the common varieties is the ice plant. It's an excellent groundcover, full of brilliantly colored flowers throughout the season. It attracts butterflies and bees and poses no harm to anyone who would touch it.

Christians can sometimes be like cacti—a mixture of thorns and beauty that keep everyone at a distance. But that's not how it's supposed to be. Are you sweet on Sunday and mean on Monday? Our dispositions should be sweet every day and not full of thorny comments or harmful gossip. Get rid of the thorns and bloom for all you're worth.

☙**In the Garden**❧ *Succulents are easy to grow and require little attention. Hen and Chicks is one of the most common, and you can find it at your local nursery. Plant a Hen in a rock garden or a sunny spot with lean soil and watch the Chicks appear.*

Heat Wave

Believers who are poor have something to boast about, for God has honored them. And those who are rich should boast that God has humbled them. They will fade away like a little flower in the field. The hot sun rises and the grass withers; the little flower droops and falls, and its beauty fades away. In the same way, the rich will fade away with all of their achievements.

James 1:9-11 NLT

In the hot summer sun, flowers take a beating. The heat sucks the moisture from their stems and petals. They wilt, and then droop. The same thing happens to the grass in the front yard. Heat and no rain eventually rob the grass of moisture. It turns brown and become stubble. The bright green is gone, as are the vivid blues of the salvia, which fade in the relentless heat. The beauty is temporary. It doesn't take long for any of this to happen.

James observes that riches humble a person and poverty exalts. Just the opposite of what we normally think. It's in God's character to display His use of the ordinary, the weak, and the obscure to bring glory to Himself.

A young shepherd named David knew about that as He faced Goliath. So did a fisherman named Peter, who dared to step out of a boat and walk on water.

When there's a healthy balance in the bank it's easy to rely on ourselves. Trusting God may not enter our minds. Money and "stuff" do not impress God, nor do they bring true security. Riches are easily lost and material possessions deteriorate over time.

Are you trusting God or relying on yourself to supply daily needs? Are you honoring God with the resources He's given you? A review of the checkbook will quickly show you where your priorities lie.

❧In the Garden❧ *Shade cloth can help protect plants from the hot summer sun. Relatively inexpensive, it's light and easily attached to frames or fences to shelter plants. Rain will go through the fabric, and it will also discourage birds.*

Profitable Pruning

He cuts off every branch of mine that doesn't produce fruit, and he prunes the branches that do bear fruit so they will produce even more.

John 15:2 NLT

But the Holy Spirit produces this kind of fruit in our lives: love, joy, peace, patience, kindness, goodness, faithfulness, gentleness, and self-control. There is no law against these things!

Galatians 5:22, 23 NLT

Pruning is necessary in any garden. Suckers take over at the base of tree trunks. They need to go because those extra branches are taking vital growth from the main trunk. Dead branches appear in bushes. Removing them gives the healthy branches room to grow. Vines get out of control and can damage structures if they're not cut back and trained. Trimming roses encourages more blooms. Pruning is part of good gardening maintenance. I collect all of the branches in my wheelbarrow and throw it into the waste pile.

Jesus expects us to be fruitful. It's the outward sign we belong to Him. The Heavenly Father prunes us with the trials of life to help us produce even more fruit. The fruit we should produce is love, joy, peace, patience, kindness, and faithfulness. That fruit is all about relationships. What do your relationships look like? Is your life full of God's peace so that your home is peaceful? Are you kind to the stranger, the store clerk? Is your love for God growing as well as your love for others? Get rid of the dead branches in your life—those bad habits and attitudes that stunt the growth of good fruit. Allow God to prune you into a vigorous, fruitful branch—one that's heavy with the fruit of the Spirit.

👐**In the Garden**👐 *The ideal time to prune away dead branches and excess growth is early in the spring before the tree leafs out. You'll see where the buds are and, more importantly, aren't, so you can trim away the dead branches. The cuts heal faster in the spring when the tree begins the vigorous growing season.*

Gardens of the Heart

Refuge

Those who live in the shelter of the Most High will find rest in the shadow of the Almighty. This I declare about the LORD: He alone is my refuge, my place of safety; he is my God, and I trust him. For he will rescue you from every trap and protect you from deadly disease. He will cover you with his feathers. He will shelter you with his wings. His faithful promises are your armor and protection.

Psalm 91:1-4 NLT

What a picture! Glancing over the courtyard wall one summer afternoon, a rare sight greeted me. A rabbit lay snoozing in broad daylight on the sand pile in the back yard. He had no concerns about hawks, coyotes, or our large Labrador that patrols the area. Granted, rabbits aren't the brightest critters, but they are, as a rule, aware of their surroundings, always ready to hop to safety. The bunny that is so low on the food chain was confident enough to sleep away a summer afternoon, cushioned on a bed of sand under the mesquite tree.

The world is full of danger on every side. The news is full of the horrible things that happen to people every day. Our stress levels climb because we fear the results of a medical test or if we'll have a job next week. Sometimes we just want to stay in bed and pull the covers up over our heads and never venture out again. We forget that we have a great place of safety if we trust our Heavenly Father whose promises are our protection.

Do you trust God for protection? Have you experienced that rest we find in the Most High alone? The rabbit slept on and hopped away safely later that afternoon. As God cared for the small rabbit, how much more He cares for us. Trust in His refuge today no matter what comes your way.

❧In the Garden❧ *Give your hands some refuge in a pair of good gardening gloves. Although there's nothing like sticking your hands in loamy earth, gloves will protect from cuts, blisters, and really dirty fingernails for those tough jobs of digging, pruning, and wrestling a shrub into a hole.*

Here Today—Gone Tomorrow

A voice said, "Shout!" I asked, "What should I shout?" "Shout that people are like the grass. Their beauty fades as quickly as the flowers in a field. The grass withers and the flowers fade beneath the breath of the LORD. And so it is with people. The grass withers and the flowers fade, but the word of our God stands forever."

Isaiah 40:6-8 NLT

Growing grass in the desert is a real challenge. It requires a lot of time and attention, which is why we have a very small patch of it. If it's not watered properly, it easily dries out in the hot southwest sun and quickly turns brown. It doesn't last long at all. Usually we have to reseed or re-sod to get it back in shape.

People are compared to grass in Isaiah 40, which is such an accurate metaphor. One day we're young, full of energy with no wrinkles. Then suddenly we wonder why we have aches, pains, and lines permanently creasing our faces. Life is over in no time at all, which is why we can't afford to waste time on things that don't last. Chasing after our youth won't bring it back. Chasing after money won't satisfy. We need to look towards things that have real value—eternal value.

God's word is eternal. It never loses its power or truth. Our bodies deteriorate, popular opinion follows the next new fad, but the Word of God is unchanging. We can stake our earthly lives on it, as well as our eternity. Don't grow more grass; grow in grace and knowledge of Jesus Christ by staying in the Word.

Memorizing Scripture is an eternal investment. You're never too old to start. It helps keep our minds sharp, our hearts spiritually healthy, and our thoughts focused on truth. Why not begin today?

❦In the Garden❦ *Make sure you choose plants suited for your hardiness zone. Most garden catalogs and many gardening websites will identify the appropriate zone on the plant. North America has 11 different hardiness and climate zones. Flowers that are unsuited for your region will only bring disappointment and more expense.*

Repurposed

Remember, dear brothers and sisters, that few of you were wise in the world's eyes, or powerful, or wealthy when God called you. Instead, God deliberately chose things the world considers foolish in order to shame those who think they are wise. And he chose those who are powerless to shame those who are powerful.

I Cor. 1:26-27 NLT

The lavender cotton plant was a mess. Once bushy and green, it was now almost entirely brown. Its appearance made the border look unsightly. It had to go. As I knelt to dig it out, a flutter of wings nearly landed me on the ground. A quail hen flew out of the plant, almost into my face. Surprised that a bird would seek shelter in the sorry looking plant, a closer inspection disclosed a hidden treasure. Nestled safely in center of the weary lavender were a dozen creamy eggs.

The worn out plant was a reminder of how I sometimes felt about ministry. There must be more qualified or more gifted people who could serve. Maybe it was time to let others take over and step back for a while. The repurposed plant reminded me that God loves to use powerless and fallible people for His work. He wants us to operate in His power alone, not relying on our own strength or wisdom to do the work.

Are you feeling inadequate about ministry? Serving can be challenging, but as long as you're breathing, our Heavenly Father has work for you to do. Sometimes the job description changes, but He enables us to accomplish the task.

Although the plant wasn't contributing to the beauty of the border any longer, it sat as a safe home for the quail hen and her eggs. The shabby lavender still had a purpose and we do too. A willing heart makes all the difference.

In the Garden *There are many varieties of lavender. English lavender is the most common. The flowers have been dried and used to scent homes and linens since ancient times. It is also used in perfumes and in medicine. Lavender oil has anti-inflammatory and antiseptic properties, and can repel insects.*

Big, Beautiful Fruit

But the Holy Spirit produces this kind of fruit in our lives: love, joy, peace, patience, kindness, goodness, faithfulness, gentleness, and self-control. There is no law against these things! Those who belong to Christ Jesus have nailed the passions and desires of their sinful nature to his cross and crucified them there.

Galatians 5:22-24

Like roses, fruit requires time and attention to get the best crop. Whether it's apple trees, strawberry plants, or raspberry bushes, they are higher maintenance than most plants. That is, if you want a good crop of apples or berries. They need pruning, mulch, the right weather conditions, fertilizer, protection from pests, and bees for pollination. The extra work is well worth the effort—strawberry jam and shortcake, apple crisp, raspberries warm and sweet popped into your mouth.

The fruit of the Spirit requires the same time and attention. We need to allow the Holy Spirit to prune the bad stuff away, like jealousy, anger, and more, which are found in Galatians 5:19-21. We need to stay in God's Word and stay away from things that draw us into sin. We need to be with other Christians and in corporate worship.

The Spirit's fruit isn't natural to us; it must be developed and nurtured. As we allow the Holy Spirit to work in us and through us, that wonderful fruit will begin to appear in our lives. Kindness, peace, self-control will all show up and be evident to others.

The strawberries are easily seen on the green plants and it's the same with spiritual fruit. It's noticed by others and by our Heavenly Father. Now that's a great shortcake!

❦**In the Garden**❦ *Strawberries are one of the most popular fruits grown in home gardens. They come in different varieties that bear in May and June or throughout the summer. Twenty-five plants can yield anywhere from 25-50 quarts. There are also varieties that do well in containers if you don't have room for a lot of plants.*

Harvest Time

Don't be misled—you cannot mock the justice of God. You will always harvest what you plant. Those who live only to satisfy their own sinful nature will harvest decay and death from that sinful nature. But those who live to please the Spirit will harvest everlasting life from the Spirit. So let's not get tired of doing what is good. At just the right time we will reap a harvest of blessing if we don't give up. Therefore, whenever we have the opportunity, we should do good to everyone—especially to those in the family of faith.

Galatians 6:7-11 NLT

When you plant summer squash, you expect nice big, yellow squash to appear after it's blossomed. When you plant string beans, long cylindrical beans are the anticipated outcome. You can't get squash from the bean plant and vice versa. If you're grumpy with the bank teller and cut off the driver that did the same to you, what kind of seeds have you sown?

The Spirit-led life looks for opportunities to do good to everyone. It's hard some days to not bite the head off the fast food worker who is slow getting your meal. It is a fast food place after all, isn't it? It's easy to greet Mrs. Jones with a sarcastic comment about her ill-behaved children in church too. The harvest from those actions is not good. It's decay and death, like the rotten tomatoes that are liquefying in the bottom of your produce drawer. They smell bad and look terrible.

The harvest of blessing is much more appealing, but we wonder if it's worthwhile when the world treats us so badly. We get discouraged, tired, and maybe a little disillusioned. Paul encourages us not to give up. Planting and harvesting are backbreaking work. But the harvest we're gathering is eternal. It's meaningful and it honors God.

Take heart, dear friend, don't give up. Ask for the Spirit's extraordinary strength to keep doing what is right. You'll have no regrets.

❧In the Garden ❧ *Native Americans called squash, beans, and corn the three sisters. These vegetables were planted together as complements to each other. The corn was tall and provided the pole for the beans to climb. The squash vine covered the ground below, giving shade to the earth, and thus prevented it from drying out too quickly.*

Help Wanted—Field Hands

When he saw the crowds, he had compassion on them because they were confused and helpless, like sheep without a shepherd. He said to his disciples, "The harvest is great, but the workers are few. So pray to the Lord who is in charge of the harvest; ask him to send more workers into his fields."

Matthew 9:36-38 NLT

There's an old saying, "Many hands make light work." I can vouch for the truth in that statement. When my siblings and I shelled peas together, we could quickly get through the grocery bags of peas my mother had picked early in the morning. If I sat there by myself, staring at four brown bags of unshelled peas, it seemed like an impossible task. There's another saying that 80% of church work is done by 20% of the congregation. It's the Pareto Principle named for Italian economist, Vilfredo Pareto who observed that 20% of the pea pods in his garden contained 80% of the peas.

Matthew observed Jesus' great compassion on the crowds who were confused and didn't know where to turn. They needed to hear the truth and they needed godly leadership. Jesus made sure his disciples knew more workers were necessary and that they needed to ask the Father, who is in charge of the harvest of souls for help. Are you working in the harvest? Are you leaving it up to someone else to share the gospel with a co-worker, a relative, a friend?

Jesus knew we'd be reluctant to work in the fields. We're afraid of what people will say, that we don't have the right words, and there's someone else who could do it better.

What if no one had shared the gospel with you? Head out to the fields today. The crowds are more confused than ever and they need to hear the truth. Ask the Lord of the harvest to send more workers to come alongside and help. The time is short.

❧In the Garden❧ *Peas are a cool weather crop, so plant them early in the spring before the danger of frost is past. When the pods are plump, harvest them early in the morning while it's cooler. The flavor is better and they retain their moisture.*

Gardens of the Heart

Waiting...Patiently

Dear brothers and sisters, be patient as you wait for the Lord's return. Consider the farmers who patiently wait for the rains in the fall and in the spring. They eagerly look for the valuable harvest to ripen.

James 5:7 NLT

Waiting isn't something I'm always good at. Maybe you can relate. Scripture tells us that Jesus is coming back and it's our job to wait for His return. It would be fine with me if Jesus came back today and took us away from all the evil, the messed up politics, and natural disasters. There are many who would quickly agree. It's easy to get discouraged, thinking that He's never coming back. Maybe Jesus didn't really mean it or it's thousands of years away.

James compares waiting for the Lord's return to the farmers waiting for the harvest to ripen. You know that beautiful big peach that dangles from the tree? It's just starting to ripen, but it's still hard and not good to eat. Some time must pass before it's really ready. You don't want to pick it until it's juicy and the flavor is peaking. You have to wait, watch, water, and keep the birds away. It's not easy to tell exactly what day it will be ready to pick.

Our Father is letting the harvest for His kingdom ripen to perfection and then Jesus will return. No, we don't know when that will be, but farmers don't stand around with hands in their pockets. They're cultivating and caring for the crop, which is what we need to be doing.

Let's care for each other and increase the Father's harvest for the Kingdom. Keep sharing the Good News while you wait. Stay in the harvest fields and keep looking up. He's coming soon.

In the Garden *Bonsai is a Japanese art form with small trees or shrubs placed in tabletop containers. Time and patient training with wires and other methods forms them into mature, miniature trees that can be enjoyed for many years.*

www.ingramcontent.com/pod-product-compliance
Lightning Source LLC
LaVergne TN
LVHW010019070426
835507LV00001B/6